DON'T STEP ON THE DUCKS

DON'T STEP ON THE DUCKS

Five Leadership Strategies for Developing Positive Relationships and Achieving Exceptional Results

Larry Kammien and Karen Evenson

Copyright © 2009 by Larry Kammien and Karen Evenson.

Library of Congress Control Number:		2009906457
ISBN:	Hardcover	978-1-4415-5060-6
	Softcover	978-1-4415-5059-0

All rights reserved. No part of this book may be reproduced or transmitted in any form or by any means, electronic or mechanical, including photocopying, recording, or by any information storage and retrieval system, without permission in writing from the copyright owner.

This book was printed in the United States of America.

To order additional copies of this book, contact:
Xlibris Corporation
1-888-795-4274
www.Xlibris.com
Orders@Xlibris.com
61160

CONTENTS

- Introduction 9
  - Getting Down to Business 13
  - Talking "DUCK"—Glossary of Terms 15

- **Guiding Principle One: Demonstrate Leadership at All Times**
  - Duck Tale: Lester and the flY Generation 19
  - Leaving the Pond: Workplace Examples 21
  - Guiding Principle Discussed 24
  - Navigating the Pond: Application of Principle 26
  - Leadership Practices 28
  - DUCKS Thought 28

- **Guiding Principle Two: Understand Your Employees' Talents, Needs, and Motivators**
  - Duck Tale: Fowl Resources and Foul Decisions! 31
  - Leaving the Pond: Workplace Examples 34
  - Guiding Principle Discussed 36
  - Navigating the Pond: Application of Principle 38
  - Leadership Practices 43
  - DUCKS Thought 43

- **Guiding Principle Three: Communicate Clear Expectations, Get Input and Listen!**
  - Duck Tale: The Duck Blind or the Blind Duck! 47
  - Leaving the Pond: Workplace Examples 49
  - Guiding Principle Discussed 51
  - Navigating the Pond: Application of Principle 54
  - Leadership Practices 60
  - DUCKS Thought 60

- **Guiding Principle Four: Keep Reinforcing Efforts, Progress, and Performance**
    - Duck Tale: You Can't Please Everyone 63
    - Leaving the Pond: Workplace Examples 66
    - Guiding Principle Discussed 68
    - Navigating the Pond: Application of Principle 71
    - Leadership Practices 74
    - DUCKS Thought 74

- **Guiding Principle Five: Scrutinize Your Results and Revise Your Approach**
    - Duck Tale: Lester's Lessons—They Aren't Corny! 77
    - Leaving the Pond: Workplace Examples 80
    - Guiding Principle Discussed 83
    - Leadership Practices 87
    - Lester's Final Thoughts 88

- **References and Sources** 89
- **Index** 91
- **About the Authors and LOS, LLC** 93

Dedication

To Greg and Ellsworth for believing in us
To all family members who supported our efforts
To leaders everywhere who inspire others to recognize their full potential

Introduction

June 2009

Several years ago while we were conducting a training class, a participant told the following joke. The more we thought about it, the more we realized that it applied directly to leadership—at its best or worst.

Three lifelong friends, Ted, Ed, and Ned, happened to die at the same time. Together they stood in front of the pearly golden gates to the afterlife.
They were greeted, "Welcome to the afterlife. You will be here with us for eternity. All of you lived good lives and deserve this reward."
The three friends were happy and anxious to continue through the gates and into paradise. They started to walk toward the entrance.
The greeter put his hand up and stopped them. "There is just one thing that you need to understand, we have a rule that cannot be broken without you suffering consequences."
"What is it?" Ted asked.
"Well, it's very simple. Don't step on the ducks."
"Ducks?" Ed repeated.
"Yes, ducks. If you step on the ducks, you will have a very harsh consequence. Can you abide by that rule?"
"No problem," Ned said confidently. The three all nodded their heads in compliance.
"Very well then," the greeter continued, "please enter." He pushed a button, and the magnificent gates swung open.
The three friends took several steps forward and stopped. There were hundreds of thousands of ducks walking around. There were thousands swimming in a beautiful lake. There were hundreds flying in the perfect blue sky. They had never seen so many ducks before.
"Who would have suspected that there would be ducks?" Ted said.
"This could be a problem," Ned said.

"We're gonna have to be really careful," Ed added nervously. "You know I'm kind of clumsy."

As if predicting his immediate future, Ed stepped on a duck after the second day. The duck began quacking loudly; then all the ducks began quacking. They were flapping their wings and creating a chaotic scene.

Suddenly a man appeared. He was wearing a long flowing white robe. In his hand was a pair of handcuffs. "Sir, I believe that you just stepped on a duck. Please extend your arm."

Ed stuck out his left arm, and one of the handcuffs was placed on his wrist.

POOF! A woman appeared, and the other handcuff was placed on her arm. The three friends stared in disbelief. Not only was this woman homely, she had the meanest mouth they ever heard.

"What's this about? Who are you? I thought I had it bad on earth. My husband was such a loser. But look at you, you make him look like a god. I want to complain to someone right now." The woman began shrieking.

The man in the robe had disappeared. Ed looked at his two friends. They shrugged and began to slink away from him.

"Whatever you do, don't step on the ducks," Ned said to Ted.

"No kidding. Man, I didn't expect that. Poor Ed."

Several weeks passed. Neither Ted nor Ned stepped on any ducks. Whenever they saw Ed, they waved. He sheepishly waved back. It appeared that the woman had not stopped complaining.

Then one afternoon, Ted was strolling by a beautiful lake. He was admiring the sky and forgot to look down.

"Quack, quack, quack." He had stepped on a duck. All the other ducks joined in.

And again the same man in the flowing white robe appeared. "Please extend your arm."

"But . . . but . . . but . . . ," Ted stammered.

"Sorry, you agreed to the rule."

The handcuff was placed on his arm, and POOF a woman was attached to the other bracelet. She was blonde with a curvaceous body and then she opened her mouth and began talking. And talking. And talking.

"Hi, like, I'm Candi. That's with an i. I love to make circles above the i. Sometimes I even draw little hearts or a happy face. Speaking of that, did you ever notice that the happy face is yellow? Don't you think that is weird? I mean, who do you know who is bright yellow?" She kept chattering without taking any noticeable breath.

Ned saw all of this from a distance. He hid behind a tree and let the new couple walk by.

Several months passed, Ned was diligent about how and where he walked. He was very proud of himself. Suddenly one day, the man in the robe appeared.

"Please extend your arm," he said to Ned.

"But I didn't break the rule," he protested.

"*I know,*" the man said.

Ned thought about it for a second. Perhaps he was being rewarded. He extended his arm.

POOF, the most beautiful woman he had ever seen was attached to the handcuffs. He stood and smiled.

"*Yes, this must be a reward,*" he thought to himself.

"*So how did this happen?*" he asked the beautiful creature.

"*I don't understand. All I did was just step on a duck,*" she replied with disgust.

Quack—quack—quack!

Getting Down to Business

Don't Step on the Ducks is designed to be a resource for new and midlevel leaders. We have written the short book in a format that allows you to read from cover-to-cover or to just read applicable sections.

There are five guiding principles that are all interrelated. To maximize the benefits of the guiding principles, we suggest the cover-to-cover approach. Our goal is to help you develop positive relations with your employees and to improve your results.

The five guiding principles are basic yet powerful. Understanding their significance as a leader is the first step to developing your skills. Applying the guiding principles will improve the morale and productivity of your employees. In addition, the guiding principles will help you avoid stepping on ducks; or if you have stepped on a duck, how you can recover and successfully navigate your business turf.

We begin each guiding principle with a "duck" tale. The stories are supported with one or more examples gathered through interviews with professionals whose experience spans decades and encompasses various industries. We then discuss the guiding principle and its application. At the end of each discussion, we provide effective leadership practices and a final thought.

By the way, we were amazed by many of the duck stepping anecdotes. As we spoke with the interviewees and recorded their stories, *we noticed that ducks are alive and well in every company*. Oh, and we also discovered that *ducks may not all look alike, but they sure do quack alike*! And *sometimes you can't even see the ducks*. But **bam**, you step on one and it begins to quack. Then they all begin to quack. And pretty soon, everyone knows that you stepped on a duck. At that point, the handcuffs or consequences appear.

Three other important things to report:

1. *Often, worse than stepping on a duck is that you may inadvertently become a duck.*
2. *Sometimes the "droppings" are also hard to avoid. They get on your shoes and smell.*
3. *And sometimes handcuffs aren't always used fairly or consistently.*

LARRY KAMMIEN AND KAREN EVENSON

In an effort to steer clear of stepping on any ducks or their droppings while compiling and writing this book, we have avoided using any names of people or companies.

Thank you to all our contributors.

And if you would like to become a contributor, please submit your tale (tail) at www.betterlos.com, and we'll post it on our website.

Talking "DUCK"

Glossary of Terms

1. **The Duck Pond**—where you work.
2. **Climate**—how it feels to work in your pond. It's based on perceptions, interactions, and management style. The climate can be a positive empowering environment, or one that is demoralizing and limits professional growth.
3. **Ducks**—people, policies/practices, issues, corporate infrastructure, decisions, strategies, and sacred cows (or ducks) in the workplace.
4. **Duck droppings**—residue left behind by the duck. A dropping is a messy situation that is the result of ducks.
5. **Stepping on the ducks**—saying or doing something which negatively impacts people and/or productivity. This can be done intentionally or unintentionally.
6. **Handcuffs**—the consequences that occur when you step on the ducks. Not everyone gets handcuffs when they step on a duck.
7. **Duck Blind**—where people hide to fire the shots. The "shots" may be policies that people hide behind to "duck" taking responsibility for a decision. "Shots" may be actions taken by someone which are career stifling for you, or they may be decisions made by upper management that disregard the feedback of the workforce.

DUCKS

Five Guiding Principles

Demonstrate Leadership at All Times
Understand Employees' Strengths, Needs, and Motivators
Communicate Clear Expectations, Get Input, and Listen
Keep Reinforcing Efforts, Progress, and Performance
Scrutinize Your Results and Revise Your Approach

GUIDING PRINCIPLE ONE

DEMONSTRATE LEADERSHIP AT ALL TIMES

- Duck Tale: *Lester and the flY Generation*
- Leaving the Pond: Workplace Examples
- Guiding Principle Discussed
- Navigating the Pond: Application of Principle
- Leadership Practices
- DUCKS Thought

At the Pond: Lester and the fIY Generation

I am a duck. I am part of the "fIY" generation—what do they call us, the millennial generation? Oh yeah, my name is Lester. I work at an ordinary pond for DD&D, LLC. (Dinner, Dessert, and Decorations). Not too big; not too small. It's a natural environment composed of individual nests that are supposed to be working together. We have the typical quack-force, although at times I feel that it is a "whack" force. It's diverse—all ages and types of ducks as well as other water fowl.

DD&D, LLC is composed of upper management (they think they're topflight), our FR (fowl resources), sales, operations, administration, IT—that has a great Web site—and all the other nests that comprise our little work world. And of course, there is a "duck blind," you know the place which is camouflaged—cleverly hidden—from where the "shots" come. They can come at any time from any direction. You usually don't even have time to "waddle or swim away."

I manage a team of three ducks in accounts receivable. We're responsible for all the "billing" of the company. It isn't my dream job, but I don't plan on staying here for my entire life. There are other ponds.

My team is composed of Wanda, Rudy, and Morris. Morris is an experienced duck who resents me because I'm so much younger. He thought that he should be promoted instead of me. He keeps reminding me of my inexperience on a regular basis. If I make a decision, he just quacks to himself and shakes his head, or he may say something like, "That's not the way I would do it."

When I ask him what he would do, he is happy to tell me in great detail. Sometimes he is right on track and points out things that I didn't consider. I thank him and let him know that I appreciate the information. Of course, then he gloats. But sometimes his way of doing things is wrong, and he doesn't like me giving constructive feedback.

I'm frustrated, and so I'm documenting my thoughts and experiences because there are times that I feel like I am going to "QUACK UP" at the office. For instance, I was supposed to get some training and mentoring when they promoted me to supervisor. That hasn't happened yet. In fact, I was thrown into the deep end of the pond—good thing I can swim! Then the first time I made a mistake, I got blasted.

Everyone makes mistakes, especially when he or she hasn't been given the basic rules. No one told me that I wasn't supposed to make certain decisions on my own. I thought the decision I made was in the best interest of my team and the business. I took full responsibility for the decision and the outcome.

(Boy, did Morris love this situation! He just kept giving me the "I could have told you" look!)

Suddenly, everyone was quacking. It seems that I stepped on two ducks—my boss and my boss's boss. And the truth is, I stepped on more than two because I evidently stepped on my own team. When they saw me get in trouble for creative thinking, it paralyzed them. They don't want to do anything without getting my approval first. I mean, now I am doing their jobs as well as mine.

I am supposed to be a leader at all times, but it isn't easy. And I can honestly say I don't know what good leadership should look like.

Quack—quack—quack!

Leaving the Pond

Workplace Example One

One of the members on the team that I led was a habitual complainer. She was also disrespectful to me and to others. She took no responsibility for her mistakes. She did the minimum work. She made frequent personal calls during work and used her computer inappropriately, including shopping online when she was supposed to be working on an assignment. Our customers asked not to work with her.

When I tried to coach her, she would either push back, admitting no wrong, or agree to the suggestions but never change her behavior. I spent much of my time documenting what she was or was not doing. Many coaching/counseling sessions followed the first. She was even put on a performance improvement plan. It was a lot of work for me, and the employee showed minimal improvement.

I thought the final straw was when she failed to attend an important meeting. When I confronted her, she said she never received notification, so it wasn't her fault. When I showed her the e-mail, which had been sent to her several days before the meeting, she said she didn't see it. Then as she got up to leave my office, she told me that she didn't feel she should have to attend meetings she considered unimportant.

I felt these behaviors fit the definition of insubordination. So I began to initiate the proper process to dismiss her. I submitted everything to my manager. The next day, he told me to back off. My manager's manager had received a call from the employee.

The employee said that she was considering going to human resources and legal. She said that I was discriminating against her because of her race, gender, and age.

My manager's manager forwarded all the information to the legal group, who suggested we should not proceed with the dismissal. Amazingly, I spent much time defending my actions. Thank goodness I had documentation.

Unfortunately, the worker was simply transferred to another group. That was the wrong solution. However, I know that I did all I was supposed to do. It was more work on my part, but I was acting as a leader. I like to think that not only did I keep my self-respect, but I also had the respect of the rest of the team.

I never discussed the worker with any of her peers. However, people could see me trying to hold her accountable for her assignments. They also were well aware of her poor work ethic and attitude, which had affected them on numerous occasions. They were greatly relieved when she was moved, but unfortunately, they lost respect for the company.

What ducks were stepped on?

Workplace Example Two

I had been in various leadership positions for seventeen years and leading this specific team for about two years. I had a good rapport with the team and a relationship built on trust. Team morale was good, and productivity was high. Things were going well. Then the inevitable happened—change! My boss left the company, and my team was put under a new manager in the organization.

A new chapter began for me and the rest of the team. We all knew the new manager and his reputation. We were really trying to see the proverbial glass half-full. I was doing my "duty" as a leader and supporting the organizational decision with the team. My new manager had never had responsibility for such an area in an organization, nor had he ever managed any of my direct reports.

Three weeks after I began reporting to this manager, the relationship began to deteriorate. It was annual performance appraisal time, and apparently, the team wasn't mine to appraise. As I completed all of the team members' performance appraisals, it was time to meet with my manager for the "blessing."

As we began to discuss the appraisals, he explained his philosophy about appraisals. It was very simple. Every person should have at least one "Needs Improvement" (the lowest rating possible) on his or her appraisal. This was very disturbing for me. I am of the philosophy that employees get the appraisal they have earned—good or bad. This discussion went back and forth for days. It ultimately ended with my manager redoing the appraisals with at least one "Needs Improvement" for each team member.

Our agreement was to disagree. You see, in the performance appraisal process, I couldn't complete it without my manager's approval on each appraisal. Oh yeah, our agreement also included him delivering the face-to-face sessions with me in the room. I could not, in good conscience, deliver a performance appraisal I didn't believe to be an accurate reflection of the full year's performance. The team knew it wasn't my appraisal of their performance. I had been giving them feedback all year long. They knew me too well.

By the way, guess who else received a "Needs Improvement" on his performance appraisal? I received it proudly! I knew I had done what was fair and just. Egg on my face—maybe. But I slept like a baby at night!

What ducks were stepped on?

Guiding Principle One

Demonstrate Leadership at All Times

Leadership. We talk about leadership on a daily basis, whether it is in our personal or professional life. But what is leadership?

For our purposes in this book, we will *define* leadership *as setting a clear direction and then positively guiding others to successfully reach the end goal.* Or in other words, leadership *is developing positive relationships and achieving exceptional results.*

Being a good leader is relatively easy when things are going well. It is when times are tough that you are challenged to demonstrate wise leadership. This means being a role model and making sure your words match your behaviors.

Based on the above definition, an effective leader demonstrates the following behaviors:

1. Assuming the responsibility that goes with being a leader ( )
2. Making appropriate and timely decisions ( )
3. Taking intelligent suitable risks ( )
4. Setting clear expectations and holding people accountable for results ( )
5. Utilizing the talents of the employees ( )
6. Communicating successfully up, down, and across ( )
7. Building trust in all levels ( )
8. Treating people fairly ( )
9. Encouraging input from others ( )
10. Giving credit where credit is due ( )
11. Projecting a positive attitude ( )
12. Losing the "I" mentality ( )

On a scale of 1-5 (one being poor and five being great), rate yourself as a leader right now. Place a number in the parentheses beside the behavior.

DON'T STEP ON THE DUCKS

In addition to the behaviors effective leaders demonstrate, they also display the following character traits:

1. Integrity
2. Courage
3. Selflessness
4. Empathy
5. Humility
6. Positive self-esteem
7. Willingness to continually learn
8. Sincerity
9. Patience
10. Willingness to admit own mistakes
11. Dedication to a greater good than self
12. Willingness to make changes

Navigating the Pond: Application of Principle

1. Review your assessment, what are your strengths?

2. What behaviors do you need to change?

3. Which character traits do you exhibit? Which of the character traits do you need to focus on as a strength? As an area to improve?

4. What would be the payback to you and your team if you made these changes?

DON'T STEP ON THE DUCKS

As a leader, you are expected to assume the responsibility and authority of your position as well as the responsibility for the performance of your team members. Therefore, accurate job descriptions and performance objectives are essential. These must be revisited periodically, revised if necessary, and communicated clearly. For a leader to be most successful, there must be a balance between responsibility and authority.

Authority. Are you an empowered leader? In your position, were you given authority with the responsibilities? Every position should have a defined level of authority. A leader needs to know the boundaries within which to operate in order to be successful and avoid stepping on any ducks. Without authority, it is simply delegation of responsibilities.

What authority do you have to make the following decisions?

- Questioning or saying no to a directive that you feel is incorrect?
- Hiring a new employee?
- Delegating daily and weekly tasks or long-term projects?
- Holding people accountable for their job performance?
- Promoting an employee?
- Determining recognition or rewards for an excellent employee?
- Terminating someone?

What support do you get from your manager when you make these decisions?

What can you do to influence management to extend your authority?

Leadership Practices:
Demonstrate Leadership at All Times

1. Ask for an accurate job description and specific objectives for yourself. (Give your employees the same thing.)
2. Clarify your level of authority with your manager.
3. Clearly define your authority as a decision maker with your employees.
4. Ask for feedback on your performance on a regular basis. What are you doing well, and what should be improved? This should be from your manager, peers, and direct reports.
5. Understand that people "liking" you is not the same as people respecting you.
6. Lead by example, and live by your values. Stand up for your team and what is right.
7. Use data to influence or persuade those above you. Be able to distinguish when it is wasted effort and when something is in your circle of influence.
8. Stand firm on what you know is right. Nobody said leadership was easy. Even if it is your boss, don't let him/her take you where you know you shouldn't go.
9. Be the Nobel Prize leader. Nobel Prize winners often try things many ways before getting it right or being awarded the prize. Reach for the Nobel Prize!
10. Choose a leader who exemplifies the behaviors and character traits that you admire. Talk to that person and ask for tips to help you become a stronger leader.

DUCKS Thought: *Leading is a privilege, respect the opportunity.*

GUIDING PRINCIPLE TWO

UNDERSTAND YOUR EMPLOYEES' TALENTS, NEEDS, AND MOTIVATORS

- Duck Tale: *Fowl Resources and Foul Decisions!*
- Leaving the Pond: Workplace Examples
- Guiding Principle Discussed
- Navigating the Pond: Application of Principle
- Leadership Practices
- DUCKS Thought

Back at the Pond:
Fowl Resources and Foul Decisions!

The sky was clear and blue. It was a quiet morning on the pond at DD&D, LLC (Dinner, Dessert, and Decorations). Its web site boasted "Don't ruffle your feathers. Let us cater your meals—from an intimate dinner for two or a large flock! We do it all!"

Bernie, the CED (chief executive duck), was thinking about the last year. "Business was doing very well. In fact, DD&D, LLC was growing at a rate of twenty percent annually. Wow, that should mean a big bonus for me," he quacked quietly to himself. "Yes, this would be the year for a nice vacation down South."

As Bernie thought back to an earlier discussion, he bobbed his head and flapped his wings. "That silly fowl resources manager, Gerald, was an alarmist. He was always quacking about some issue."

"I think that we have some real problems with morale," Gerald quacked excitedly. "We need to conduct a climate survey to see how ducks feel about working at DD&D."

"Climate survey? Look around you. The weather couldn't be any better!" Bernie said and began flapping his wings.

"I mean, how employees feel about their jobs."

"They should be happy to be working here. We continue to grow at a rapid pace. Not every company on the pond is doing as well. The problem is that we had three bad managers."

Recently, DD&D, LLC had a 100 percent turnover in its top three executives. Bernie didn't bother to question the exits, he just rationalized the three ducks had never really fit into the culture. So it was time to bring in some "real" talent.

"Just because they left doesn't mean they were poor at their jobs," Gerald said.

Bernie dismissed the thought with a shake of his head.

Reluctantly, FR had lined up some interviews. Bernie decided to conduct them himself. He made his decisions and hired Ernie, Gertie, and Birdie for the three top positions—a butcher, a baker, and a candlestick maker, as he liked to refer to them—although no one else thought the titles were funny.

Bernie may have had his head under water during the interviews. He didn't bother to listen to anyone. He simply read the résumés and asked questions that confirmed what he thought.

"Would you like to work for a fast growing company? We need ducks with a commitment to results. But of course, I know I can trust you to do what it takes, right?"

All three candidates nodded their heads in agreement. Bernie was very excited; he supposedly hired the best in their fields. They were excellent swimmers, they could quack with the best, and they all had quite a bill of goods to boast.

In reality, the only experience Ernie actually had regarding being a butcher was running from one so he didn't become dinner.

Ernie thought of himself as a great manager—what was so tough about that? You told employees what to do, refused to accept questions or ideas, and then continually checked up on the underlings. Bernie liked that style of management.

Gertie didn't say she could bake, she said her life's goal was not to be baked. And if the truth was told, her former director reports that most of Gertie's ideas were half-baked. She continually changed her mind and then didn't communicate the changes. Gertie's style of management was to let employees alone. She wanted them to like her and hated conflict.

And when Bernie asked Birdie about her candlestick experience, she puffed out her breast feathers with pride and gave a dissertation on her background as a CED for a candelabra company. She saw great things for DD&D and wanted to implement some new ideas and thinking. Bernie was a little intimidated but decided Birdie would settle down once she had the job. She had a great résumé.

Ernie began managing the way he had always managed. His new job and team required a different approach, but Ernie refused to change. He felt he didn't necessarily need to know anything about the company or his division; ducks on his team began flying the "nest." When he was counseled about the poor results, he became very defensive and vowed to drive his team even harder.

DON'T STEP ON THE DUCKS

Gertie struggled but refused to ask for help. She wasn't sure what her role and responsibilities really were. She refused to make large or small decisions. She didn't hold employees accountable, and consequently her team's productivity and results began slipping. Some members of her team began to sabotage efforts to make Gertie look bad.

Birdie was experiencing job dissatisfaction as an overqualified, undermotivated employee; her new ideas were constantly rejected by Bernie. She began regretting her departure from the last company. Compared to DD&D, the old company looked much better.

Within six months, the three executive ducks came to Bernie with their resignations. This duck was cooked So much for the vacation in the South.

Quack—quack—quack!

Leaving the Pond

Workplace Example One

In the corporate world, one reward for success is being given more responsibility and work. Unfortunately, being successful at one position doesn't make you successful at another. At some point, people may be promoted to their level of incompetence.

A leader who was very successful in his assigned responsibilities was rewarded with a promotion. With the promotion came more responsibility. However, the responsibility was in an area of the company that was not familiar to this leader. Rather than acknowledging his lack of expertise in this new area, this leader chose the cookie-cutter approach—watch out, baker! His theory was, whatever made him successful before would make him successful again.

Without analyzing the situation, without gaining a complete and accurate understanding of the new responsibilities, and without considering the team members, he continued in the same mode of operation. This approach resulted in an unmotivated team feeling frustration and resentment. Ultimately, the team started to disband.

In this leader's eyes, all was still successful. He thought he was simply weeding out the weak team members. For every departure, there was a rationalization of how the person just didn't fit. There was never a concern about the climate created by the leader.

Unfortunately, in the short-term, this leader was viewed a success (in his eyes and potentially, in the eyes of some of those above him). In the long-term, he was a failure as a leader.

What ducks were stepped on?

Workplace Example Two

A concept that has become very popular and deemed highly effective is team-based interviews. Many companies will form interview teams to meet with candidates when there is an open position.

My company was no exception. We were to use team-based interviews for all open positions. Unfortunately, there were leaders who followed the process but didn't heed the advice of the interviewers.

It's pretty simple to imagine the situation: interview teams are put together, multiple interviews take place with multiple candidates, and then consensus-based discussions take place among the interviewers. It's an easy process to follow. The result: a candidate is selected for the position and hired. Hold on—not so fast! That's how it worked, except for the hired part. In this case, higher management stepped in, selected and hired a different candidate.

I believe it goes without saying, the team was very discouraged. This sent a clear message about the value of their input and where the power resided in the group.

What ducks were stepped on?

Guiding Principle Two

Understand Your Employees' Talents, Needs, and Motivators

Proper talent management is more than a popular HR phrase. It is an approach to leading a team to reach exceptional results. Proper talent management is especially important in a twenty-first century's diverse workforce. Motivating and engaging employees with various elements of diversity is a challenge that all organizations, therefore leaders, are facing.

Effective leaders recognize and understand their own strengths and leverage them. They surround themselves with a diverse group of employees who complement them, in effect, they become a broker of talent.

In other words, leaders do not have to be great at all things. However, leaders must be good at adapting to their diverse teams. They have a responsibility to find the avenue for relating to each team member's work style, communication style, and learning style. They also need to determine each individual's motivators.

One instrument that is internationally recognized and can be utilized at an individual contributor level is the *Insights Discovery Personal Profile*. This is an instrument that provides details into personal effectiveness about you, as an individual, and about your interaction with others. When utilized with an intact work group, it allows for excellent team analysis in regard to the strengths and opportunities for the team based on the Insights® model.

The foundation of the model is developed from the work of Carl Jung's personality preferences, also found in the *Myers-Briggs Type Indicator®*. However, Insights provides much greater detail in a more user-friendly and memorable format.

As a leader, you can move to the next step, *Insights Discovery Transformational Leadership Profile* and *Insights Navigator Transformational Leadership Profile*. The first of these advanced instruments utilizes information from your *Insights Discovery*

Personal Profile and generates a leadership perspective. The second of the advanced instruments is enhanced with a 360-degree feedback tool.

The leadership model consists of four manifestations: results, visionary, relationship, and centered leadership. The following brief descriptions will help you gain a perspective on these manifestations:

- *Results leadership* encompasses strengths around agile thinking, delivering results, and leading change.
- Some strengths of *visionary leadership* are creating a compelling vision, communicating with impact, and again, leading change.
- *Relationship leadership* shares the strength of communicating with impact and adds fostering teamwork and facilitating development.
- Finally, dimensions of strengths for *centered leadership* include facilitating development, leading from within, and agile thinking.

The same dimensions may not appear as strengths for each manifestation. Some may be more innate for each of the leadership manifestations. However, each of these dimensions is important in an effective leader.

(Insights, Insights Discovery, and the Insights Discovery Wheel are registered trademarks of the Insights Group Ltd. All references to copyright materials or trademarks owned by the Insights Group Ltd are reproduced with their kind permission. Insights Discovery and Insights Learning Systems were originated by Andi and Andy Lothian)

Navigating the Pond: Application of Principle

- Utilize an assessment tool to determine preferences and motivators of your team members.
- Complete the *Insights Discovery Personal Profile* evaluator to enhance your self-awareness.
- Schedule and participate in a team session for *Insights Discovery Personal Effectiveness Program.*
- Develop a plan to utilize your team more effectively.
- For a more advanced look at the impact of your leadership style, participate in the *Insights Discovery Transformational Leadership Program.*

Diversity

"The great organization must not only accommodate the fact that each employee is different, it must capitalize on these differences. By changing the way it selects, measures, develops, and channels the careers of its people, this revolutionary organization must build its entire enterprise around the strengths of each person" (Buckingham and Clifton 2001).

Workplace diversity has been experienced in the more traditional areas such as culture, gender, age, religion, etc. However, generational diversity is a newer phenomenon. For the first time in the United States, we have four generations in the workplace. This provides many learning opportunities because differences can be experienced in communication, values, work ethic, perceptions, and expectations, to name a few.

But to define diversity properly, remember diversity is also about similarities. Oftentimes, focus on diversity in organizations is about differences. This type of focus tends to create a negative perception of diversity. By including similarities in the definition, we neutralize the negative perception of differences. Differences are just differences!

Diversity is only one component of talent management critical to an organization. Other components are recruitment, selection, development, and succession planning.

Recruitment

An effective recruitment process, along with the selection process, is essential. *It is much easier to hire the right candidate than to terminate the wrong candidate.* Therefore, candidate sourcing is an important first step. Companies and leaders need to determine the best sources for their industry, requirements, and long-term goals. Remember to keep the company mission, vision, and values in mind when determining recruitment sources and candidate selection.

Leaders should

- work closely with their human resources representatives throughout the entire recruitment, selection, and hiring process;
- know the sources for recruitment in their organization;
- know the job requirements and interview appropriate candidates;
- hire the best qualified candidate for the position.

Selection

Many companies utilize behavior-based interviewing during their selection process. It is a popular type of interviewing due to the typically positive outcomes. Behavior-based interviewing questions inquire about past behaviors. The theory behind this type of interviewing is that past behavior is a predictor of future performance. To make it most effective, interview questions should be based on job competencies relating to job responsibilities and the skills, knowledge, and abilities necessary to perform the job. All of this should be tied to a competency model developed for the company.

Sample questions:

Tell about a time you had to deal with an angry customer.
Give an example of a time you had to coach an underperforming employee.
Tell about a time you provided a reward or recognition for an employee.

Leaders should

- know their company's competency model;
- identify those competencies that are important for success in the open position;
- hire the best candidate for the position, not an overqualified or underqualified person.

Development Planning

One tool used, in some format, by many companies is the development plan. They can have a variety of titles such as Individual Development Plans, Personal Development Plans, or Employee Development Plans—to name a few. These plans should be based on skill, knowledge, and ability gaps as measured against the job requirements. Again, the development opportunities should align with the company's competency model.

Leaders should

- identify job competencies for each position;
- identify job roles and responsibilities;
- clearly communicate each person's role and responsibilities;
- create a development plan for each employee;
- determine appropriate training and other development opportunities;
- discuss openly and listen to the employee's input regarding his/her talents and skills.

Succession Planning

Succession planning is a process used by organizations, which provides a pipeline of qualified candidates to fill leadership positions in each area of a business. It aids in identifying depth of talent, readiness of high potential talent, and plans for the succession of the identified talent.

The process can include such steps as workforce planning, gap analysis, and leadership development. In addition to identifying the succession of positions in the company, succession planning can help identify needed positions in the workforce and the skills and abilities for those positions. This process does not have to be confined to the top levels in a company. Each leader can conduct the succession planning process for their areas of responsibility including their position. Leaders should ask themselves who are they developing to assume their position as they move up in the company.

If a succession planning process is designed well and utilized properly, it can also help identify the low performing positions and lead to addressing these issues. The process used, design of the measurement tool or matrix, and the timing should be defined by each company. Some of the factors influencing these decisions may be turnover rate, availability of qualified candidates, and growth of the business. However, the succession planning process should be conducted at least once a year.

Leaders should

- know their company's succession planning process;
- partner with their human resources representative to facilitate this process within their teams;
- determine their career goals within the organization;
- identify potential employees to fill their position;
- develop employee's talents.

Navigating the Pond: Application of Principle

1. Revisit each of the "Leaders should" points and determine your opportunities for development.

Leadership Practices: Understand Your Employees' Talents, Needs, and Motivators

1. Companies invest a lot in people so get the most for your investment. Make your return bigger—utilize people for their full potential.
2. Don't allow yourself to be enamored by hiring someone with qualifications above those required for the job. You won't be able to keep them motivated, interested, challenged, or employed!
3. Preparing thorough job descriptions based on job-task analysis work will help you hire right. Every time a position opens, re-examine the job description and requirements. Make sure the job really is what's advertised. If it quacks like a duck, it is a duck.
4. Utilize structured interviews based on the competencies required for the job. Make the fit right for you and the employee. Don't hire a baker to do a candlestick maker's job.
5. Don't let resource allocation drive employee development. (Don't kill the "duck" that lays the golden egg!) When you are working with less people, it is imperative to make sure that they have the skills necessary to do the job.
6. Conduct team building exercises using tools that help people understand and appreciate similarities and differences. Refer to the discoveries in your meetings and discussions.
7. Respect people who are different from you—you are not perfect. What is the impact that your style is having on others?
8. Growing other leaders is part of your job. When people are ready to be promoted, make sure you are their strongest advocate. Use a structured form of succession planning.
9. Remember, a leader is only as successful as his/her team.
10. Manage up—model the behaviors that you would like to see your manager use. When your team has successes, tell your boss and your boss's boss. Influence with data.

DUCKS Thought: *Leaders are only as good as those they develop!*

GUIDING PRINCIPLE THREE

COMMUNICATE CLEAR EXPECTATIONS, GET INPUT AND LISTEN!

- Duck Tale: *The Duck Blind or the Blind Duck!*
- Leaving the Pond: Workplace Examples
- Guiding Principle Discussed
- Application of Principle
- Leadership Practices
- DUCKS Thought

Back at the Pond:
The Duck Blind or the Blind Duck!

Four ducks were flying toward the pond. Arnie, the leader, shouted over his right wing to his team. "It looks all clear to me, does anyone see anything suspicious?"

"I don't," *said Reba who was flying directly behind Arnie. Reba agreed with Arnie at all times.*

"Wait, I think I do see something. Is that a duck blind with hunters off to the left?" *Fred asked cautiously.*

"Yes, and those ducks sitting on the water look like decoys," *Aretha quacked.*

"What's the matter with the two of you, it looks fine to me," *Arnie said, obviously ignoring their observations and advice.*

"Let's land." *He and Reba started downward, feet pointing toward the water.*

BAM! BAM! BAM! *The shots echoed.*

Luckily, all four ducks escaped although Reba did lose some tail feathers.

"Boy that was close," *Arnie quacked as the four ducks flapped their wings furiously to gain altitude and speed.* "What pond do you think we ought to try now?"

"Why ask us?" *Aretha quacked.* "You didn't listen and almost got us killed."

Arnie appeared to be confused by the comment.

"Yeah, you decide. We'll circle while you go in for a landing at the next pond," *Fred said quietly.*

LARRY KAMMIEN AND KAREN EVENSON

"Does my butt look big without my tail feathers?" Reba asked.

Quack—quack—quack!

Leaving the Pond

Workplace Example One

Senior management asked the director of our group to develop strategies around each of the product lines for which we had a responsibility. She delegated complete responsibility to us, but as usual, communicated limited details.

While she was gone, we discovered from other groups that their directors were working on the task with them. We also realized there were specifications communicated by senior management, which had never been given to us. Consequently, we had to redo some of the work we believed to be completed.

Frustration and aggravation comes in many flavors (would you like a sugar cone or a waffle cone with that?).

Precious time was wasted as we discussed the director's poor leadership.

There was resentment because we felt the director believed our other assigned work wasn't as important as this project (assigned to her by senior management).

We also agreed the director would redo much of the finished product when she finally reviewed it (based on history) and then not communicate any changes to us.

There was also the haunting notion she would present it to senior management as her work (maybe the justification would come from her changes to the group's work).

Whew! At least we didn't get to thirty-one flavors!

By the way, this obviously wasn't the first time such a behavior occurred on this director's part. As a result, most of our group began job searches. Turnover is so expensive.

What ducks were stepped on?

Workplace Example Two

Innovation. The word is in every journal and annual report. It has become the mantra for the twenty-first century. I totally embrace the concept that innovation is fundamental to every company's present and future. Unfortunately, my boss didn't see the value.

Our company jumped on the bandwagon several years ago. Upper management informed us that one of the strategic initiatives for that year and beyond was applying innovative thinking in every area of our company. Recognition programs were created. What upper management failed to do was explain what they meant by innovation and how leaders should actually encourage it.

When my manager returned from one of the meetings, his directive to us was, "We are supposed to be innovative. I personally don't think there is anything wrong with the way we are currently conducting business, but you're supposed to come up with new ideas that can make us more cost-efficient and productive. So if you have any ideas, just write them down and give them to me. I'll look over the idea and see if I think it has any merit."

Wow! What a motivating speech. But because I wanted to improve our workplace, I immediately began writing down some ideas. I actually had been thinking of them over time. I even went one step further, I didn't just give the idea, I showed an implementation plan and the money and time that would be saved.

I forwarded my ideas via e-mail to my manager and waited for some response. A week went by without even an acknowledgment that the e-mail had been received. I decided to ask my manager.

"Oh, yeah. I got the ideas. I just haven't had time to read them yet. I didn't expect anyone to come up with things so quickly. I'll get back to you."

Another week went by, and then an e-mail reply showed up in my mailbox. "Sorry, but your ideas don't fit into our budget this year. They aren't exactly what we're looking for."

I asked for a meeting to explain the ideas and understand the reason for dismissing them. I was told the subject was closed.

What ducks were stepped on?

Guiding Principle Three

Communicate Clear Expectations, Get Input, and Listen

Let's start by looking at the two key phrases in this guiding principle. First, *communicate clear expectations*. Three words come to mind: communication, organization, and prioritization.

Communication

There is never a time you are not communicating. Communication is the method you use to interact with others. Effective communication is reaching understanding between people not necessarily reaching agreement. That means you are responsible for the message you are sending in addition to making sure the receiver understood it as intended. And as the receiver of the message, you are responsible for clarifying our understanding.

We know 93 percent of our communication is nonverbal. That 93 percent is made up by 55 percent body language and 38 percent voice. Only 7 percent of the message is words (A. Mehrabian 1981). With more and more electronic communication being used, much of the message may be lost. Ninety three percent is missing in text messages and e-mails, while 55 percent is missing in telephone conversations.

No matter what method or tool (phone, pager, e-mail, text messages, face-to-face) you use, basic principles apply.

Create and Send Effective Messages

- Consider the receiver of the message—what does s/he knows about the information and what does s/he need to know?

- Be specific in your content. What do you want the receiver to do with this information?
- Be careful not to give too many details at once.
- Organize the information—think in terms of an outline.
- Choose the proper medium for delivering the message—telephone, e-mail, texting, or face-to-face.
- Check for feedback to make sure the message was understood as you intended it.
- Use spell and grammar check for written messages. Remember, spell-check does not catch every error.
- Consider the receiver and his/her needs.
  - Use words they will understand.
  - Evaluate the emotional state of the receiver.
  - Use safe rather than harmful words/phrases.

Harmful Language

Harmful language is composed of words or phrases that offend or evoke negative emotional responses. Although using harmful language is usually done inadvertently, a simple word or phrase can cause some unintended damage; the conversation goes downhill very fast.

Examples of harmful language:

- What's the problem now?
- You never.
- Here we go again.
- I'll get to it when I have the time.

Safe Language

Safe language is composed of words or phrases easily understood and not easily misinterpreted. Safe language considers the receiver's emotions. Safe language is specific. It focuses on the data and depersonalizes the problem.

Examples of safe language:

- I understand.
- I need your help.
- I am sorry about the delay, etc.
- Let's take a look at the requirements of the task.

DON'T STEP ON THE DUCKS

Use Active Listening

- Stop speaking and doing other activities and focus on what is being said.
- Make eye contact.
- Ask questions to clarify.
- Paraphrase and repeat the message.
- Use nonverbal cues such as nodding to indicate to the speaker you are paying attention and you understand the message.
- If the message is being sent by e-mail or text message, don't try to interpret the emotions, ask the sender.
- Read the words and confirm your understanding of the message by paraphrasing in your response.

Navigating the Pond: Application of Principle

1. What are some communication barriers you and your group face?

2. What is the impact of these barriers? How do you prevent them?

3. What single thing could you do to improve your communication?

4. Give two examples of harmful language. Now change the examples into safe language.

Organization

In today's work world, employees are expected to do more with less. The less may include less financial, less physical, and/or less human resources. If you are being asked to accept a greater number of tasks and projects, it is even more important for you to use an organized approach to work.

Do you consider yourself to be an organized person?

- What tool do you use to track appointments as well as tasks?
- How often do you plan?
- How often do you monitor and change those plans?
- How do you communicate the changes?
- How do you manage the tasks that fill up your time?
- What is the impact on you and others if you're not organized?

Prioritization

Priorities. Who creates them? How often do they change? In most workplaces, the priority of a task may come from a higher level than you. And the priority may change daily (sometimes even more often).

- Before you assign a task to someone, you need to understand what the task is and its priority.
- Establish the time sensitivity of the "task" (i.e., is it urgent, requiring immediate attention?).
- Consider the importance of this task in regard to other tasks that need to be completed, and prioritize from the most important to the least. Ask why this task is important, Is this the first step in a process? Who is deeming it as important?
- Communicate the importance to the person performing the task. And if priorities change, tell the person what has changed and why! Don't expect him/her to read your mind.

Ask for Input and Listen

When do you need to get input from your employees? The correct answer is *constantly*. Asking for input is one way to keep employees engaged. Engagement is measured in what employees think, how they feel about the organization, how they act, or the effort and energy exerted. They need to feel that their opinions and ideas are not only considered but actually implemented.

Employee involvement and engagement is a foundational piece of the effective business pyramid. Employee engagement leads to improved employee satisfaction and quality output. This, in turn, increases positive productivity, which directly contributes to improved customer satisfaction. And when customer satisfaction grows, markets expand, and profits multiply.

Effective Business Pyramid

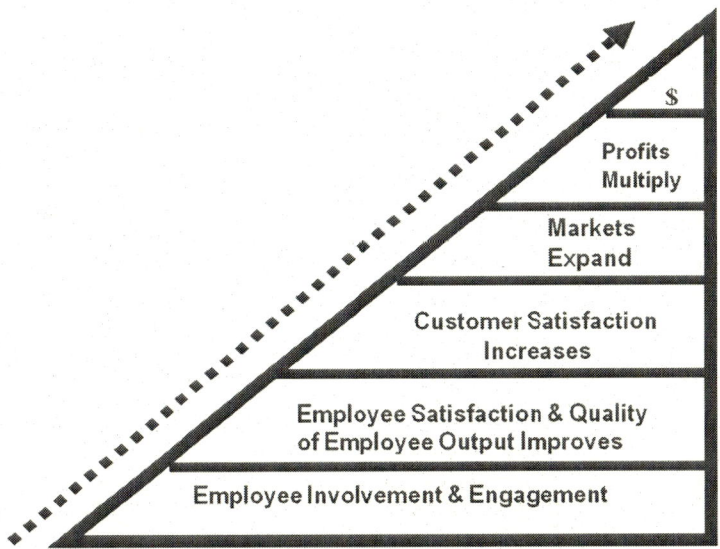

A good leader is always asking for input around decisions and problem solving. This is not to say that all decisions should be made by a team. If you determine a decision needs to be your decision, then make it alone.

If you ask for input, don't disregard it. Asking for input and then ignoring it is detrimental to your credibility and reputation. It also damages morale and trust. And it guarantees that people won't be willing to give input in the future.

As the leader, you must be willing to listen to ideas and to take responsible risks. Safe leaders continually follow the same path or squelch new ideas. This limits opportunities and growth. There is a way to manage and minimize risk.

After people have generated and presented their ideas, ask the following questions:

1. What is the return on investment—money, people, costs, etc.?
2. What is the impact—who, when, how—long or short term?
3. Does this idea meet our standards around safety, benefits, legal, etc.?
4. Do we have the knowledge to implement or do we need outside sources?

(Evenson 2004).

Allow people to answer these four questions. A "No" response or negative response doesn't mean that the idea is not good or viable. The group or person may need to reassess and make some adjustments. If the answers are all positive or justified, then the group has information to carry forward and use to persuade the decision maker(s).

There are times that you may need to reject an idea. If so, give the person or group a prompt answer, the reason for rejecting the idea, and suggest how they may change it to gain acceptance.

If you accept the idea, ask the individual or group to create a plan of implementation and monitoring. And the most important thing, if the idea is good or great, give credit where credit is due. Don't present the idea upward as if it was your idea.

Think before you act and speak. Even in the times of panic, crisis, and overload, a leader has to carefully think through a situation. Plan before you act or speak. Consider the what-ifs of any situation. Bounce your thoughts off a peer, advisor, mentor, or coach. Get another perspective. Everyone doesn't see things your way!

Leaders should

- determine who it is you admire most as a leader (in or out of the organization) and build a mentor/coach relationship;
- utilize a trusted peer to seek a different perspective on an issue;
- spend a day once a month with one of your employees while doing their job.

DON'T STEP ON THE DUCKS

Navigating the Pond: Application of Principle

1. How do you solicit and use input from your employees?

2. What are the benefits of asking for input?

3. How can you encourage collaboration with your team?

4. What is the current culture concerning risk taking?

5. Evaluate a current idea and apply these four measures:

    - ROI
    - Impact
    - Standards
    - Knowledge

Leadership Practices: Communicate Clear Expectations, Ask for Input, and Listen

1. Use effective communication in both giving and receiving messages. Check for understanding on the part of the employee.
2. Make sure you are organized and understand the urgency and importance of the tasks that you are delegating. If you don't understand, ask questions to clarify.
3. Help people prioritize the importance of the tasks that are to be accomplished.
4. Explain what needs to be accomplished, why it should be done, and when. If there is a specific way that the task must be completed, explain that also.
5. Communicate any changes that have been made and discuss the new plan.
6. If you want more employee engagement, then ask for their input!
7. Encourage innovative thinking and empower employees to work together collaboratively. Give people the tools and time to do creative problem solving.
8. Give credit where credit is due.
9. Take responsible risks.
10. Determine what decisions are yours and take responsibility.

DUCKS Thought: *How a leader listens is more important than how often s/he speaks.*

GUIDING PRINCIPLE FOUR

KEEP REINFORCING EFFORTS, PROGRESS, AND PERFORMANCE

- Duck Tale: *You Can't Please Everyone!*
- Leaving the Pond: Workplace Examples
- Guiding Principle Discussed
- Application of Principle
- Leadership Practices
- DUCKS Thought

Back at the Pond: You Can't Please Everyone

Let me tell you about what happened last month. I remember having a hard time meeting an unrealistic deadline. We weren't goofing off, just the opposite. Everyone had been working long hours trying to get the project done. I decided to discuss this with my boss, Yolanda.

"We need more time to get this done," I said to Yolanda.

"Oh, that could be a problem," Yolanda quacked. She flapped her wings like she always does when she gets nervous or upset. "Perhaps we just need a different approach."

"I don't think it is our approach. I told you about my concerns last week," I said as respectfully as possible. "And what about the storm we've been experiencing? Rain has been pouring down all day, the wind is so strong that we can't fly, and those noisy geese flew in and basically took over the entire west end of the pond."

"Well, some of those things just aren't preventable. You are a very determined young duck, Lester, and I believe in your ability."

"I appreciate that, but it's a deadline that just isn't realistic. We can have it completed tomorrow. I have the data to show you what I mean."

"Okay, I understand. I have a meeting with Richard, I'll explain," Yolanda promised after reviewing all the information I provided.

She swam toward the corner nest and settled into her place around the lily pad. She swallowed hard and began quacking, "Richard, before we start discussing other things, I need to let you know we aren't going to make the deadline. The storm—"

"I don't want any excuses. I told you to get it done. The storm is not my problem," Richard quacked and paddled in circles. His green head bobbed up and down.

"The storm put us behind. We can have the work completed tomorrow," Yolanda responded nervously.

"Get it done today. If I would have wanted it tomorrow, I would have said so."

"But my team—"

"Obviously, you just don't drive your team hard enough," Richard said firmly.

"I don't think that's what is needed," Yolanda answered quietly.

"You know this attitude is going to be reflected in your performance review."

After the meeting, Yolanda swam back to our nest. She asked my team to meet her.

"How did it go?" I asked anxiously.

"I appreciate the effort you've given. The timeline hasn't changed so we need to figure out what it is going to take to get this finished," Yolanda said.

"Magic—that's all that will help!" Wanda quacked.

"I could have told you Richard wouldn't extend the deadline," Morris said and shook his head. "He wants us to fail."

"I don't want failure. I want you to be successful. Let's start by sitting down and reviewing exactly where we are. Then let's brainstorm what we need, from other ducks, tools, our knowledge, and others."

"Shouldn't we just work instead of trying to brainstorm?" Morris asked.

"Yolanda is right. Let's reorganize our approach, taking five minutes to regroup and plan could save time later," I said.

DON'T STEP ON THE DUCKS

"That's the spirit, Lester. Let's get started. I'm committed to staying here and working alongside all of you."

I guess she could have dumped on us and flown away. Instead, she said the right things to foster morale and productivity. However, her actions with Richard didn't really show support. Maybe she just didn't want to step on that duck.

By the way, we missed the deadline by just a few hours. Richard was not happy, and he let us know of his disappointment.

Our group talked about how to be more proactive in light of all the barriers we had encountered. We identified those we could have predicted and prevented and those we couldn't control. And we all agreed, sometimes even when you do your very best, it may still not hit the mark.

"I could have told you," Morris said.

Quack—quack—quack!

Leaving the Pond

Workplace Example One

I worked for a man who felt it was perfectly acceptable to yell at people and call them names. He would do it either publicly or in a private session. He used belittling language and aggressive hand gestures.

He made threats, "I'll make sure you never go any further in this company."

The man was a bully.

I spoke with coworkers about his behavior. They all agreed he was creating a hostile work environment. They also agreed we needed to take action.

I went to his boss and spoke to her about his behavior. She agreed that, at times, "he did go over the top. But there was no reason to take this any higher, like to HR or legal." She said she would speak to him about his behavior and thanked me for bringing it to her attention.

Not long after that conversation, when I did something he perceived as "wrong," he called me at my home. It was Saturday morning. He began to yell. I told him I would not tolerate the language he was using or the behavior he was demonstrating. I said if he wanted to speak with me, I would meet him on Monday morning to have a rational discussion. We had a very tense meeting on Monday. Nothing was really resolved. He refused to listen although he was not as aggressive.

Several weeks later, his boss notified me; I had been reassigned. "We have to reduce headcount and reorganize the department. We have found a position for you at X. We feel it is an opportunity which will allow you to coach others, including your new boss."

"Do I have a choice?"

"Not really, but believe me, this isn't a punishment."

The new assignment was a dumping ground for employees who all had stepped on ducks. Unfortunately, the handcuff wasn't just the demotion but also the new boss. She had no leadership experience and was mean-spirited. She did not listen and was never organized.

By the way, the bully was never moved or demoted.

What ducks were stepped on?

Workplace Example Two

I'm reminded of a manager I worked for twenty years ago. It's amazing how you don't forget those things, which affect you negatively. They linger long in your mind.

I used the term *manager* instead of *leader* because there is quite a difference. This individual was a manager because his focus was on controlling and managing what people did and how they did it. He never developed strategies or built plans with the team.

He had been moved to another position due to lack of performance. However, the performance issue was never addressed. Upper management thought it was easier to move him and provide some lame explanation. Of course, he could see right through the smoke being blown around the issue.

When a person is "demoted" or moved to another position (with no real explanation), the wind is sucked out of his sails. The motivation to do their best work everyday and inspire others to do the same is diminished.

Struggling with his own disappointment, frustration, and anger, he built it right in to his management style. He managed the team in a controlling manner (he was going to ensure performance was up to expectations this time). He knew how to do everything and the right way to do it. But he didn't stop there. He went one step further. He decided he needed some "victories" for senior management to see. So he presented all ideas and work as his own. There was no sharing of the successes. No credit was given—only taken. When there was "limelight," he was in it.

As you can imagine, there was almost 100 percent turnover in the team. And much to his dismay, the manager was let go in the next reorganization.

What ducks were stepped on?

Guiding Principle Four

Keep Reinforcing Efforts, Progress, and Performance

Let's go back to our definition of *leadership—setting a clear direction and then positively guiding others to successfully reach the end goal.* The key part of the definition at this point is GUIDING others to reach the end goal.

You've assessed the diverse talents of your workforce. You know what motivates your team and self. You've communicated clear expectations and encouraged input. Now you need to hold your employees accountable and guide them to reach those expectations. And the way to guide people is to *coach and develop them.* Developing people is one of the most important contributions that you can make as a leader, and it is one of your responsibilities.

Coaching is not a new concept. The sports world has been using it for centuries. Think of coaching as a leadership tool. It's individual attention from an expert to unlock a person's full potential and/or to remove a blind spot (Logan and King 2001). So coaching is not a one-time event. It is an ongoing process that requires time, patience, and effort. Yet it can also be very rewarding for a leader.

Skill, knowledge, and motivation need to be considered when assigning tasks or assessing performance. The following table uses the categories A, B, C, and D. These are dynamic. People can move from one category to another based on the situation. Before coaching, determine what category describes the employee, then use the appropriate coaching techniques.

DON'T STEP ON THE DUCKS

Employee	Ability/Motivation	Coaching Tactics
Employee A	This employee has both the ability and motivation to do the task that is assigned. He/she is eager to achieve and likes what he/she is doing.	• Clarify expectations and allow the employee to perform. • Talk about future development opportunities. • Use as a mentor to other employees. • Document good performance.
Employee B	This employee has the motivation to do the job but is missing the skill set to do the task assigned.	• Clarify expectations and skills necessary. • Provide appropriate training. • Monitor skills. • Team up with an employee A. • Document training and progress.
Employee C	This employee has the skill set and ability but lacks the motivation to accomplish the task assigned. There are various reasons why a person is not motivated (i.e., bored, personal issues, burned out, etc.)	• Clarify expectations and skills. • Uncover reason for lack of motivation (talk to the person). • Determine appropriate solutions. • Hold employee accountable. • Document lack of completion.
Employee D	This employee lacks both the ability to do the job and the motivation. He/she may have previously been an A, B, or C employee. However due to a change either in or out of his/her control, he/she has transitioned to a D employee. No one should ever start as a D.	• Clarify expectations and skills that are necessary. • Determine if the employee has the capability to do the job. • If not, then consider assignment to another task. • If the capability is there, provide proper skills training. • Monitor skills, retrain if necessary. • Hold employee accountable. • Document progress (or lack thereof).

Assess each of your employees as an A, B, C, or D. Create a matrix, and evaluate your employees' skills, knowledge, and abilities versus the job requirements. Are they appropriately aligned?

Job Requirements	Skills, Knowledge, and Ability	Team Member Assigned	Assessment	Development Initiative
• Complete the weekly billing of customers	• Access to information • Computer ability	• Paula	• Limited skills on computer software	• Provide proper training on computer software

Discuss with the employee and then create a development plan. Determine appropriate training and other development opportunities, monitor progress on a regular basis, and hold employee accountable for results.

When management chooses to avoid their responsibility of addressing performance issues, there can only be one result. It's like two trains traveling opposite directions on the same track. The result is predictable and inevitable. It's just a matter of when it will happen—based on the speed of the trains.

When you assign a task or project, people accept the responsibility to complete that assignment. Once they have accepted the responsibility, you can then hold them accountable for the results. If you have set the proper expectations that include why, what, when, and how, you have a plan that can be monitored. You must have the employee's confirmation of the expectations and his/her agreement to take action. Without employee buy-in, the desired outcome will be compliance not commitment.

Once you have the employee's confirmation, turn the task over and monitor the progress. Monitoring and checks should be done on a regular basis. Depending on the employee you are working with (A, B, C, or D), you may do more or less monitoring. Please remember that active and appropriate monitoring is not micromanaging.

Navigating the Pond: Application of Principle

1. Why is it important to continue to coach an *A employee*?

2. Give an example of when you were a *B* employee.

3. What could a leader do that may contribute to an *A* employee becoming a *C* employee?

5. What may contribute to an *A*, *B*, or *C* employee becoming a *D*?

Recognition and Reward

The final part of this guiding principle concerns recognition and reward. Addressing these three simple topics at a job interview may give insight concerning the prospective employee. Asking your current employees for their answers to the three topics is critical.

1. *Define recognition.*
2. *Define reward.*
3. *What makes you want to stay with a company?*

Individuals in all four generations (matures, boomers, Xs, and millennials) have different motivators. Be careful not to categorize the generations simply by age, dig deeper. For some people, job security is a fundamental motivator while for others it may be about power or personal achievement. For many people, work-life balance is critical. Some people like public recognition. Others are very happy with a thank you from his/her manager. Some people like the reward of promotion. Others want their performance rewarded monetarily. Regardless the motivation, all employees want the system to be fair and equitable and meet the individual's needs.

When should you use recognition? When you believe the reinforcement of a behavior will cause the person to repeat that behavior to add value to the organization. Some examples may be

- when an employee has gone over and above the expected performance,
- when an employee has met expectations and displayed a positive attitude,
- when an employee has attempted a new skill (taking a risk) but has not yet met the desired outcome.

Recognition must be sincere and specific. Be wary of overutilizing a reinforcer. When a reinforcer becomes saturated, the reinforcement value is lost.

DON'T STEP ON THE DUCKS

Navigating the Pond: Application of Principle

1. What types of recognition do you currently use? Are they providing the expected outcome?

2. What other types of recognition could you add to your tool box?

Leadership Practice: Keep Reinforcing Efforts, Progress, and Performance

1. Coach your employees not as a one-time event, but as an ongoing process.
2. Praise their progress and effort even if the result isn't exactly right. Then regroup and plan to prevent future failures.
3. Reassess the current skill set of employees and reassign responsibilities as necessary. Remember, where someone started is not necessarily where they currently are in their career. If you have the wrong ingredients, you end up with duck soup!
4. Provide the proper tools, resources, and training.
5. Monitor without micromanaging.
6. If the employee is veering off course, correct immediately. Remind him/her of the responsibility he/she accepted.
7. When priorities change, communicate the change and rationale immediately.
8. Acknowledge good performance on a regular basis. People respond to positive feedback and are willing to make adjustments more willingly when they aren't defensive.
9. Discuss recognition and rewards—determine what motivates each individual.
10. Create recognition systems that are effective.

DUCKS Thought: *Leadership is not a title, it is a series of well-defined actions.*

GUIDING PRINCIPLE FIVE

SCRUTINIZE YOUR RESULTS AND REVISE YOUR APPROACH

- Duck Tale: *Lester's Lessons!*
- Leaving the Pond: Workplace Examples
- Guiding Principle Discussed
- Application of Principle
- Leadership Practices
- Lester's Final Thoughts

Back at the Pond One Last Time: Lester's Lessons—They Aren't Corny!

Lester sat among the reeds eating his simple lunch of corn. The year was coming to an end, and he was feeling depressed.

Bedford swam up next to him. "Do you mind if I eat with you?"

"No, feel free."

"You look down—no pun intended," *said the more experienced duck. He laughed at his own joke and then began eating his lunch of stale bread with great enthusiasm.*

"I guess that I am."

"How are your results?"

"I think fine."

"How are your ducks performing? Are they all in a row?" *Another inside joke that set up a new round of laughter.* "Sometimes I just quack myself up!"

"They're doing okay."

"Do you have a climate of high trust? Do your ducks feel as though they are all treated fairly and equitably?"

"I haven't heard any complaints about fairness."

"They may not quack about anything, but you may see it on their faces, or in their actions or lack of action. Have you noticed any ruffled feathers? You have to read all the signs—verbal and nonverbal. How do you measure the performance and results?"

"Well, basically, if we get the job done on time," *Lester answered.*

"When I was just starting to manage, I found that I always kept my head down, just looking at the water where I was swimming. If it looked clear, then I thought everything was fine. I responded to the algae or cloudiness of the single spot. What I found I needed to do was start looking at the whole pond and the banks of the pond and even the sky."

"Why?" *Lester asked.*

"Because if you're just managing to the moment, then you will just get through until the next moment. If you look to the end of the day, the week, and beyond, then you start leading."

"I guess I just don't understand," *Lester said.*

"You need to look at the big picture and see how all the components fit together. Hey, when a storm is coming, there are many signs. The wind picks up, the water begins to get choppy, the temperature begins to change, ducks or geese may be making a racket or even leaving. If you wait until the first drop of rain hits the surface, it may be too late to take cover."

"But how do I look at the big picture when I have so much to get done today?"

"That's a question leaders have been asking for a real long time."

"And have they come up with the answer?" Lester asked.

"I don't know about others, but I kind of figured that if I follow some basic leadership principles, I'll have more time to look at the big picture and be spending less time on all the daily tasks."

"So what are these principles?"

"DUCKS," Bedford said, obviously proud of himself.

"Ducks? What kind of answer is that? I am a duck and I don't know what you're talking about."

"D stands for demonstrate leadership at all times. U is understand your employees' strengths, needs, and motivators. C is about communicating clear expectations, getting input, and listening. The K is to keep reinforcing efforts, progress, and performance. And finally, S stands for scrutinize your results and revise your approach if necessary."

"That makes it easy to understand and they really are just common sense. Thanks," Lester said.

"Oh, one last thing," Bedford said as he began to swim away. "Watch out for the duck blind!"

Quack—quack—quack!

Leaving the Pond

Workplace Example One

During a company reorganization, imagine that in the corporate world today, I began reporting to a new manager. I had some interaction, ever so brief, with this individual previously. It was very positive, so the relationship started off on a good note—you might say we were in "tune!" Until the trust word reared its ugly head. One day, in a discussion about the future of the group, my manager brought up the *T* word. Yes, he broke the barrier and opened the discussion on trust.

Basically, the discussion from his point of view was simple. He said, "You trust people too much."

I had to let those words echo in my head a few times before I could formulate any response. And, when I did, it was profound.

"What do you mean, I trust people too much?" I didn't even know how to respond to that statement.

After a fairly lengthy discussion, it came down to different philosophies. His was "*Don't trust people until they prove to you they should be trusted.*" Mine, on the other hand, was "*Trust people until they prove to you they should not be trusted.*"

What a dichotomy! His was based on loyalty to himself. Mine was based on loyalty to others, or well, trust. You can only imagine where the relationship went from there—or can you?

Fairly soon thereafter, I made a mutually agreed upon move in the organization. It was definitely for the better. My former manager and I were both happier and maintained a productive working relationship.

There is some irony that came out of this issue. Prior to me moving on to another position, we had conducted a survey on the leaders in his organization. My feedback was very positive (his was not so positive).

As he shared the feedback with me, he stated, "I don't know what you do as a leader, but the people that report to you love you."

I can't say I know exactly either. But I am willing to bet trust has something to do with it!

What ducks were stepped on?

DON'T STEP ON THE DUCKS

Workplace Example Two

I'm reminded of a leader who had a great deal of impact on me, mainly because she was one of the first corporate leaders in my career. She had been in the corporate world for twelve to thirteen years. She had always worked for the same company and in the same department. She had worked her way up to the manager of the department.

In some ways, she had a positive impact on me. She was very knowledgeable, had worked every job in the department, and had a very strong work ethic. She was dedicated to producing results.

On the flip side, she showed me some things that weren't so positive too. She had no work-life balance, she spent many evenings and weekends in the office, she had a lot of baggage (because of her longevity in the department), and she was struggling with burnout (although I am not sure she recognized it).

It took me some time and experience to sort these things out, I was young and green and wasn't sure which behaviors were right for me. I simply saw she was being rewarded for the department results.

One observation had more impact on me than the others; it was her attitude about the work, the company, and the people. She seemed to always be unhappy and frustrated—maybe even angry. I am not sure she intended this projection or was even aware of it. But the impact on the team was powerful. The attitude spread like wildfire! The message was that it was okay to be short with people, to treat them poorly, and that verbal complaining was acceptable. The team dynamics and the climate were neither pleasant nor effective.

What ducks were stepped on?

LARRY KAMMIEN AND KAREN EVENSON

Workplace Example Three

Cut costs. In fact, the corporate edict was to cut ten million from the budget. No, not just my small group, but also everyone in the corporation was part of the initiative.

Meeting after meeting was held to determine how to reach that point. My team as well as others came up with many cost-saving ideas that were implemented. Not satisfied with the results the company was getting, upper management made the first of many bad decisions. They decided to eliminate all overtime.

The company was already working at a personnel deficit. There had been a hiring freeze for over a year. When people left the company, their positions were not filled. The staff that remained was assuming all the tasks. Overtime was not something we "used" indiscriminately. We weighed the options and then approved the additional hours when necessary. Several levels of management scrutinized each of those decisions, so it made no sense to arbitrarily eliminate all overtime.

When the employees found out, they were outraged. They felt as though they were undervalued and underappreciated. They were tired and stressed, and they were ready for mutiny. There was an unspoken work slowdown. Absenteeism and accidents increased as productivity decreased. The mess left behind in the workplace because of the decision cost more money to clean up than it ever saved.

A few months later, the "no overtime" was lifted. The news was not received with gratitude. In fact, many people declined the overtime when offered. That meant productivity remained down. Because of my loyalty and dedication to the company and my team, I worked seventy hours a week to meet our deadlines. Funny thing, I was salaried so I never received any overtime pay for those additional hours nor did I receive any recognition.

I started looking for a job. I couldn't keep myself motivated, much less my workforce. The stress is just too much. I had a constant internal struggle between my high expectations and standards for myself and others versus my frustration and disappointment in the system.

What ducks were stepped on?

Guiding Principle Five

Scrutinize Your Results and Revise Your Approach

The last principle is as important as the first four. It is about self-awareness. It is about having the courage to look at you and ask some tough questions.

- Am I a leader that others can respect?
- Do I lead by example or by default?
- Do I need to make some changes in my approach?
- Would I follow me?

It is critical that you continually assess your performance as a leader and get feedback from your manager, peers, and direct reports. You can use a formal 360-degree feedback survey or have informal conversations with each of the groups. But before you do, take a look at the climate you have created as a leader.

Climate is the perception of how it feels to work in a particular environment. It includes a complex mixture of norms, values, expectations, policies, and procedures that influence individual and group patterns of behavior.

If the climate is one of low trust, it will be very hard to get honest feedback about your performance.

Build a Climate of High Trust

Trust is at the heart of every relationship. Building it does not happen quickly. But unfortunately, trust can be damaged or destroyed quickly.

"Society approaches change on the false assumption that every extra increment of effort will produce a corresponding improvement in result. In truth, improvement does not correspond directly to effort. Small changes can have huge effects. It all depends on when and how the changes are made. Similarly, with trust, all of the so-called small things we do to build trust eventually reach a threshold where high trust explodes and cascades. Reaching the tipping point lies in the persistence in doing those small things in getting to the threshold" (Gladwell 2000).

These are some indicators of low trust in the workplace:

- Sabotage
- Poor quality
- Employee turnover
- Lack of customer loyalty (poor sales)
- Employee thefts
- Abuse of sick leave
- Decreased productivity
- Alienation from work
- Lack of loyalty
- Delays in action
- Nobody telling anyone else what's going on
- Feeling undervalued
- Attitudes such as "I just work here" or "Ask the boss"

What are the costs to you and the company?

Trust Assessment

Define *trust*.
Based on your definition, how would you rate the level of trust:

	Poor	Fair	Average	Good	Excellent
Between you and your direct reports	1	2	3	4	5
Between you and your peers	1	2	3	4	5
Between you and your manager	1	2	3	4	5
Between you and your customers	1	2	3	4	5

Now that you have assessed the trust in your relationship, how would others define and assess it? Ask them and have an open conversation about the results.

Five key leadership behaviors which can build trust are as follows:

1. Treat people fairly.
2. Maintain confidentiality.
3. Be true to your word and honor your commitment.
4. Lose the "I" mentality.
5. Convey the right attitude.

Treat People Fairly

How many times have you said or heard someone else say, "That's not fair"? Fairness is a measure people use to judge others' actions or decisions. It is usually based on the individual's personal biases, assumptions, and/or experience.

Ask your employees to define *fair*. You may be surprised at their answers. They usually include, "everyone has to pull their weight," "no favorites," "decisions should consider people's needs," or "communication is always one way," etc.

It often happens; leaders have those employees whom they see as star performers. Hopefully, they have based their decision on fair and equitable performance measurements and not the "I like that person" or "they agree with everything I say" criteria. It happens even to the best leader.

The basic concept to remember is this: favoritism—whether real or perceived—is detrimental to any organizational climate.

In order to better understand the implications, think of short-term versus long-term results. In the short-term, if a leader "favors" a team member, that individual produces results (of their own and from their direct reports if they have any). In the long-term, the individual continues to produce results while the rest of the team members' results begin to diminish. Over time, the results of the team continue to decline or you begin to have turnover in personnel. Without fail, this will be the eventual result.

You have a responsibility, as a leader, to evaluate and reward employees fairly and equitably. Your personal biases need to be left out of the process. This helps produce effective leaders. It may not be easy, but it is critical.

Maintain Confidentiality

Employees may confide personal information to you. Maintaining confidentiality is a critical leadership behavior for building trust. However, in certain legal or safety situations, a leader may have to breach that confidentiality. In these cases, the leader needs to communicate this to the individual prior to sharing the information with the appropriate parties. And remember, a leader never discusses one employee with another employee.

Be True to Your Word and Honor Your Commitments

Can people count on you? Are you good for your word? Do you live up to your commitments? How would others respond to these questions regarding you? Perception is reality. It is not whether you believe you are being true to your word or honoring your commitment, it is what others believe that impacts your credibility. If you make a commitment, deliver on it. If you can't, communicate the rationale.

Lose the "I" Mentality

As a leader, you have to be willing to accept the responsibilities that come with the position regardless of the circumstances. Wanting to be a leader is about more than power or status. It is about influencing an organization, driving to achieve results, and motivating and developing people.

Leadership isn't about being the best at everything and making the most money. It is about developing individuals to perform to the best of their ability and become future leaders (if they so desire). It is about creating a synergy so the overall performance of the team far outweighs the performance of all the individuals combined.

Being an effective leader can provide a sense of pride and contribution. But that comes when you lose the "I" mentality and begin thinking "we."

Convey the Right Attitude

Remember as the leader goes, so goes the team. Be careful what attitude you project to the team. There's a good possibility it will become the team's attitude. Your team members will be looking for you to take the lead (hence, the term *leader*!) on how to respond, communicate, and present yourself in a professional manner. So before you display a negative attitude to your team, hit the pause button. Remember, it's not just about you anymore. You are the example for the whole team!

Attitude is usually conveyed by your actions and words. People judge others based on the behaviors they see. They do not always know the other person's intent.

As a leader, you must consistently project an attitude of "can-do." It doesn't mean you will always agree with things or even support decisions handed down. During those times, it is easiest if you tap into the ideas of others to accomplish a task. Better to ask, "How can we get this done?" than to say, "This is impossible."

Leadership Practices: Scrutinize Your Results and Revise Your Approach

1. Define and assess the level of trust in your relationships.
2. Get feedback through a formal 360-degree instrument or through conversations.
3. Regularly review your last performance appraisal for areas of improvement and maintenance of your strengths.
4. Decide what you would like to work on (don't try to change too much at once).
5. Discuss with your manager a list of results to achieve.
6. Create a plan and communicate to the appropriate people.
7. Implement the plan.
8. Get feedback on how the plan/change is working.
9. Revise if necessary, implement again.
10. Give yourself credit for your leadership successes.

Lester's Final Thoughts

I'm getting ready to sign-off. Before I join the rest of my flock, here are some key thoughts for new leaders.

1. Being a leader is not easy.
2. Leading can be frustrating yet very rewarding.
3. Remember, the most important responsibility of a leader is developing people.
4. Building positive relationships and achieving exceptional results takes time, patience, persistence, and continual learning.
5. Leadership is earned not granted.
6. Often times, the most effective leading is done beside people and not in front of them.

References and Sources

Recommended Reading

Blanchard, Kenneth H., and Paul Hersey. 1977. *Situational Leadership*. Bank of America.

Blanchard, Ken, and Marc Muchnick. 2003. *The Leadership Pill*. New York: The Free Press.

Buckingham, Marcus, and Donald O. Clifton. 2001. *Now, Discover Your Strengths*. New York: The Free Press.

Collins, Jim. 2001. *Good to Great: Why Some Companies Make the Leap and Others Don't*. New York: HarperBusiness.

Evenson, Karen A. 2004. *Redefining F.E.A.R.: Maximizing Limited Resources with Unlimited Ideas*. Hiliton Head Island: Cameo Publications.

Franklin Covey. 1997. *Building Trust, The Key to High Performance*. USA: Franklin Covey Co.

Friedman, Thomas L. 2005. *The World is Flat: A Brief History of the 21st Century*. New York: Farrar, Straus & Giroux.

Gladwell, Malcolm. 2000/2002. *The Tipping Point*. New York: Back Bay Books/Little, Brown and Company.

Hamel, Gary. 2007. *The Future of Management*. Boston: HBS Press.

Logan, David, and John King. 2001. *The Coaching Revolution: How Visionary Managers Are Using Coaching to Empower People and Unlock Their Full Potential*. Avon: Adams Media.

Pink, Daniel H. 2005. *The Whole New Mind: Why Right Brainers Will Rule the Future.* New York: Riverhead Books.

Insights® Learning & Development, 7700 Chevy Chase Drive, Suite 1.230, Austin, TX 78752

Insights® Instruments:

- Insights Discovery Personal Profile
- Insights Discovery Transformational Leadership Profile
- Insights Navigator Transformational Leadership Profile

INDEX

A

authority, 27–28

B

business pyramid, 56–57

C

climate, 83
coaching, 68
communication, 51
company competency model, 40

D

development opportunities, 40, 70
development planning, 40
diversity, 39
   generational, 39
duck blind, 19
Duck Pond, 15
DUCKS, definition of, 78
duck tales
   "Lester's Lessons—They Aren't Corny!," 77
   "Lester and the flY Generation," 19

E

effective messages, 51
employee categories, 68–69
Employee Development Plans, 40. *See also* development planning
employee engagement, 56, 60
   active listening, 53
   asking for inputs, 56

F

favoritism, 85

G

gap analysis, 40. *See also* succession planning

H

harmful language, 52

I

"I" mentality, 86
Individual Development Plans, 40. *See also* development planning

innovation, 50
Insights model, 36
   Insights Discovery Personal Profile, 36, 38, 90
   Insights Discovery Transformational Leadership Profile, 36, 90
   Insights Navigator Transformational Leadership Profile, 36, 90

J

job security, 72
Jung, Carl, 36

L

leadership, 24, 28, 68
   character traits of a leader, 25
   key leadership behaviors, 85
   commitment, 85–86
   fairness, 85
   maintaining confidentiality, 85
   right attitude, 86
leadership development, 40. *See also* succession planning
leadership model
   centered leadership, 37
   relationship leadership, 37
   visionary leadership, 37

M

Myers-Briggs Type Indicator, 36

O

organization, 55

P

Personal Development Plans, 40. *See also* development planning
prioritization, 56
proper talent management, 36

R

recognition, 72
recruitment, 39
   candidate sourcing, 39
reward, 72

S

safe language, 52
selection, 39
   behavior-based interviewing, 39
self-awareness, 83
skill set, 74
story of Ted, Ed, and Ned, 9
succession planning, 40–41

T

trust, 83
   indicators of low trust, 84
   trust assessment, 84

W

workforce planning, 40. *See also* succession planning

The Authors and LOS Partners

Larry Kammien's and Karen Evenson's professional careers include working for and with major corporations, nonprofit organizations, and government agencies. They currently lead and direct a successful private consulting company, LOS, LLC, with clients from diverse industries in the United States, Great Britain, Europe, and China.

Their understanding of common workplace issues and human needs creates a positive connection with their audiences. Their delivery style is dynamic and humorous. Their presentations educate people of all ages and professional levels on timely issues and motivate the participants to achieve their full potential.

- Accreditation: Insights into Personal Effectiveness
- Certifications: Insights Transformational Leadership; KAI; PDI Profilor
- Qualification: MBTI

LOS Philosophy

Leadership & Organization Solutions is a private consulting company that focuses on strategic leadership and organization development.

The LOS philosophy is that high performance companies recognize that they do not need to choose between profits and people. They know who they are and who they're not. And their leaders hold true to the company's values and culture at all times.

LOS Services

Customized Leadership Retreats (1-4 days)

- Event Planning
- Customized Seminar: L.O.S.T.™ Culture
- Strategic Assessment and Planning
- Team Building Exercises

- Executive Coaching

Leadership Consulting

- Culture and Climate Assessments
- Customer Evaluations
- Readiness for Change
- Strategic Planning
- Talent Management
- Executive Coaching
- Creative Problem Solving

Instructional Design and Delivery of Corporate Training

Leadership

- Transform Your Culture: L.O.S.T. ™ The Leadership Compass
- Strategic Thinking: Change Management is an Oxymoron
- Navigating the Political Pitfalls: Don't Step on the Ducks
- Leadership Thinking: The Next Level

Human Resources

- Talent Management: The Collapse of the Corporate Ladder
- Engagement and Empowerment: Letting Others Lead
- Diversity and Inclusion: The Workplace of Today and Tomorrow

Creative Problem Solving

- Redefining FEAR

Effective Communication

- The Power of 26 Letters
- Presenting for Positive Impact

Keynote Speeches

- The 3 Rs of Engagement©
- The Workplace of Today and Tomorrow
- The Collapse of the Corporate Ladder
- The L.O.S.T.™ Culture

DON'T STEP ON THE DUCKS

- When the Weather Inside is Frightful
- Change Management is an Oxymoron
- Don't Step on the Ducks©
- Leading through FEAR
- Creating and Sustaining Positive Connections

For information about our services, visit our website: www.betterlos.com